THE SCIENCE OF A SHIPWRECK

LISA AMSTUTZ

Published in the United States of America by Cherry Lake Publishing
Ann Arbor, Michigan
www.cherrylakepublishing.com

Consultants: Neal Lopinot, Director & Research Professor, Center for Archaeological Research, Missouri State University;
Marla Conn, ReadAbility, Inc.
Editorial direction: Red Line Editorial
Book design and illustration: Design Lab

Photo Credits: Shutterstock Images, cover, 1; Frank O. Braynard Collection/AP Images, 5; Raymond Wong/National Geographic Image Collection/Glow Images, 6; National Geographic Society/Corbis, 8, 17; Dorling Kindersley/Thinkstock, 11, 12, 18; North Wind Picture Archives, 15; Department of Antiquities/AP Images, 21; Adept Technology, Inc./Globe Newswire/AP Images, 22; US Coast Guard, 27, 29

Library of Congress Cataloging-in-Publication Data
Amstutz, Lisa J., author.
  The science of a shipwreck / by Lisa J. Amstutz.
    pages cm. -- (Disaster science)
  Audience: Age 11.
  Audience: Grades 4 to 6.
  Includes bibliographical references and index.
  ISBN 978-1-63137-627-6 (hardcover) -- ISBN 978-1-63137-672-6 (pbk.) -- ISBN 978-1-63137-717-4 (pdf ebook) --
ISBN 978-1-63137-762-4 (hosted ebook)
  1. Marine accidents--Investigation--Juvenile literature. 2. Shipwrecks--Juvenile literature. I. Title.

  VK199.A47 2015
  910.4'52--dc23   2014004033

Cherry Lake Publishing would like to acknowledge the work of
The Partnership for 21st Century Skills. Please visit www.p21.org
for more information.

Printed in the United States of America
Corporate Graphics Inc.
July 2014

ABOUT THE AUTHOR

Lisa Amstutz specializes in nonfiction for children. *The Science of a Shipwreck* is her eighteenth book, and her work has appeared in a variety of magazines as well. Lisa enjoys learning fun facts about science and history to share with kids. Her background includes a bachelor's degree in biology and a master's degree in environmental science.

TABLE OF CONTENTS

CHAPTER 1
THE *TITANIC* DISASTER...............4

CHAPTER 2
HOW SHIPS FLOAT 10

CHAPTER 3
HOW SHIPS SINK...................14

CHAPTER 4
STUDYING SHIPWRECKS...............20

CHAPTER 5
MAKING SHIPS SAFER...................26

TOP FIVE WORST SHIPWRECKS 30

LEARN MORE 31

GLOSSARY 32

INDEX...32

THE TITANIC DISASTER

As long as people have traveled by sea, there have been shipwrecks. One of the most famous happened in 1912: the sinking of the *Titanic*. Its builders called the ship "practically unsinkable." Sixteen watertight sections inside its **hull** could be sealed off if needed. Up to four of them could flood without sinking the ship. Bands played and crowds cheered as the huge ship pulled away from the dock in England for its first voyage.

At the time it was built, the Titanic was considered one of the safest, most modern ships in the world.

Disaster struck four days into the journey. The night of April 14, 1912, was dark and calm. The *Titanic* steamed ahead. By the time Captain Edward Smith's lookout spotted an iceberg in the ship's path, it was too late. The iceberg tore into the ship's hull and the *Titanic* began taking on water.

The crew began loading the lifeboats, but the lifeboats could only hold about half the ship's passengers, who totaled more than 2,200. In the confusion, many lifeboats were launched only partly full. Only about 700 people got into the lifeboats, even though the lifeboats could have carried nearly 500 more people. Some passengers wearing life jackets jumped from the sinking ship into the icy water. Many froze to death before help could arrive. Nearly three hours after hitting the iceberg, the ship tilted upward and then snapped in two. Both halves plunged to the ocean floor.

The dramatic destruction of the Titanic *shocked the world.*

How could this have happened? Survivors told their stories and court hearings were held. But no one knew for sure exactly how much damage had been done to the ship's hull. Some of the details would not be filled in until after the wreck's discovery in 1985. Today, scientists continue to study the *Titanic* to learn more about what happened that night and how to prevent it from happening again.

For thousands of years, people have built boats for fishing, travel, and trade. The oldest shipwreck ever found dates back to 2200 BCE, more than 4,200 years ago! It lies near the coast of Greece. There are likely many older shipwrecks that have not been found. People in boats settled islands such as Australia tens of thousands of years ago. Some of these ships likely sank. These early wrecks have probably **decayed**, making them difficult or impossible to find. In all, experts believe there are more than 3 million shipwrecks on the world's ocean floors.

In the days before airplanes and cars, ships were considered fast, safe ways to travel. Mountain ranges were

The ancient Greeks relied on the sea for transport and trade. Many of their boats likely lie on the ocean floor today.

hard to cross by foot or on horseback, and robbers attacked travelers on land. Travel by sea had its own dangers, and those early ships sank for many reasons. Among them were poor design, storms, overloading, warfare, fire, attacks by pirates, and the lack of good maps and navigation tools, which caused ships to strike rocks or **reefs**.

As explorers ventured further into the world's seas and oceans in the 1500s, sailing technology improved. Still, early ships were largely limited by the winds that pushed their sails. In the 1800s, steamships came into use. Unlike previous vessels, steamships did not need wind to move them. However, their steam power introduced new problems. Furnace fires and boiler explosions caused many disasters.

Modern ships run on diesel fuel and electricity. Sailors have accurate maps and high-tech tools to find their way. They can radio for help. Stricter safety laws have made ships safer as well. Despite these advances, shipwrecks still occur. Even with modern technology, mistakes can be made. In 2012, one century after the *Titanic* sank, the *Costa Concordia* passenger ship ran aground when the captain guided the ship off course. Thirty-two people died, and the ship was destroyed.

CHARTING A COURSE

Today, maps and computers help sailors reach faraway destinations and avoid dangerous rocks and reefs. Early explorers had no idea what lay past the boundaries of their maps. They used the sun and stars to navigate. They watched for signs of land, such as floating vegetation and shorebirds.

— CHAPTER 2 —

HOW SHIPS FLOAT

It may be hard to imagine how an object weighing more than 92 million pounds (42 million kg), such as the *Titanic*, can float. The ancient Greek scientist Archimedes figured out the basic science behind how ships float. Archimedes' principle explains the concept of **buoyancy**. The principle states that the force pushing up on a ship is equal to the weight of water the ship pushes out of the way. In other words, the *Titanic* pushed 92 million pounds (42 million kg) of water out of the way to stay afloat.

10

Archimedes is well known for his many contributions to math and science.

The secret is in the shape of what you want to float. If you put a block of metal in water, it would quickly sink. But when you stretch out that metal and fill it with air, it pushes water out of the way over a larger area. Distributing the weight like this allows a boat to float. Engineers use lightweight, sturdy materials to build ships. They must spread the weight of the ship evenly across its hull. A strong, straight **keel** keeps the ship stable.

WEIGHT AND BUOYANCY

The shape of a boat and the weight it is carrying are important factors in whether it will float. What is the difference between the diagram in the middle and the diagram on the right? Why does the boat float while the raft sinks? Identify the keel. What might happen to this boat without the keel?

The hulls of large ships are often shaped like large rectangles with rounded edges. These edges let the boats slide more easily through the water. Their hulls ride lower in the water than those with *v* shapes. Ships with rectangular hulls are less likely to tip over and more likely to give passengers a smooth ride. Today's ships often have watertight compartments inside their hulls. These can be sealed off if they start to flood, preventing water from spreading to the rest of the hull.

ARCHIMEDES' PRINCIPLE

Archimedes of Syracuse lived in ancient Greece more than 2,200 years ago. He was a talented mathematician and inventor, and he made many important observations about water and buoyancy. The development of his theories about buoyancy began when King Hiero II asked Archimedes to figure out whether his crown was pure gold. While taking a bath, Archimedes thought of a way to do this. He noticed the water rose and splashed out when he got into his bath. This led him to understand the basic concepts behind displacement, which he could use to measure volume.

Archimedes conducted an experiment. He carefully measured how much water the crown displaced. This gave him the exact volume of the crown. Archimedes then divided the weight of the crown by its volume to find its density. He discovered that the crown's density was different than the known density of gold. This meant some cheaper metals had been added to the crown, and it was not pure gold. The finding led Archimedes to do more experiments and make more discoveries about buoyancy.

How Ships Sink

Many different factors can cause shipwrecks, but the most common is water entering the hull and sinking the ship. With the *Titanic*, an iceberg broke open the hull. In the case of the *Nuestra Señora de Atocha*, a jagged reef sliced a hole in its hull as it headed from Cuba to Spain in 1622. A storm drove the ship, which was loaded with treasure, into the reef. It quickly sank. Very rarely, a collision with a wild animal can sink a ship. A sperm whale brought down the *Essex* in 1820. The ship was on a

The survivors of the Essex *sinking lived for months at sea before their rescue.*

whale-hunting expedition when the whale rammed it. The impact tore open the ship's hull and it soon sank.

Ships can also sink following collisions with each other. The Italian ship *Andrea Doria* sank in 1956 after colliding with another ship in the fog near the coast of Massachusetts. The ships saw each other on their **radar**, but the crews were not trained enough on the radar equipment. They could not tell exactly how far away the other ship was. The *Stockholm* plowed into the side of the *Andrea Doria*, carving out a 30-foot (9 m) hole. After the disaster, radar training was improved.

Many ships are intentionally sunk during wars. The deadliest shipwreck in history happened during World War II (1939–1945), when a Soviet submarine sank the German passenger ship *Wilhelm Gustloff*. Approximately 9,400 people died.

Not all ships are sunk by holes in their hulls, however. Powerful winds combined with an unstable design to sink the *Mary Rose* in 1545. This ship belonged to King Henry VIII of England. The ship's crew set out to fight the French navy in the English Channel, the body of water between England and mainland Europe. After firing its cannons on one side, the *Mary Rose* turned sharply. A gust of wind caused the ship to tilt at a dramatic angle. The top of the ship was too heavy, making it unstable in the sea. Water poured into its **gunports**, and the *Mary Rose* sank.

Some ships sink because they are loaded too heavily. Their weight overpowers the buoyancy that keeps them afloat. In 1876, British politician Samuel Plimsoll

After it sank in the English Channel, the wreck of the Mary Rose *was not discovered until 1971.*

suggested that every ship should have lines on the hull showing when the ship was loaded to a safe level. These lines are often called Plimsoll lines. Laws require that ships not be loaded past these lines. However, overloading still occasionally happens. In 2012, the Russian cargo ship *Amurskaya* sank after being overloaded with gold ore. The *Swanland* sank in 2011 due to overloading and a rusty hull.

PLIMSOLL LINES

There are many standard Plimsoll lines. They show how deep a ship should sit in the water based on the water conditions. Ships can float higher or lower depending on the salt content and temperature of the water. This is because these factors change the water's density. Based on the lines shown here, can you tell how salt and temperature affect the way ships float?

TF: Tropical fresh water
F: Fresh water
T: Tropical seawater
S: Summer temperate seawater
W: Winter temperate seawater

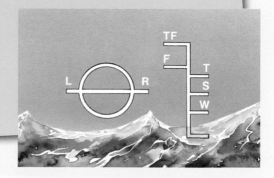

People sometimes sink old, unused ships on purpose to form artificial reefs. These make good fishing spots and interesting sites for **scuba** divers to visit. First, workers remove oil and other chemicals from the old ship. They take out valuable parts such as copper wiring. Then they cut openings in the hull so divers can enter. After the ship has sunk, living things such as coral, barnacles, and algae grow on it and attract fish and other sea life.

THE SINKING OF THE *TITANIC*

Although hundreds of survivors saw the *Titanic* sink, many questions about the condition of the wreck remained. The survivors told very different stories. Some said the ship sank in one piece, but others thought it broke in two. No one knew how much damage the iceberg caused. Most believed it must have torn a huge gash.

The truth about these questions remained a mystery until Robert Ballard and Jean-Louis Michel discovered the wreck in 1985. Their photos of the site showed that the ship had indeed broken in two. The two halves lay about 2,000 feet (600 m) apart on the ocean floor. Although the front looked nearly intact, the back was badly damaged. In 1996, a team of scientists visited the *Titanic* to learn more. They went down in a submarine called *Nautile*. They used a special type of **sonar** to see through the mud that covered part of the ship. What they found was surprising. Instead of a long gash, there were only six small slits in the hull. Some were no wider than your finger.

STUDYING SHIPWRECKS

In addition to helping us understand when and why ships sank, studying wrecked ships can teach us more about the people who sailed them. For example, dated bricks found on an unidentified wreck off the coast of Florida proved that it could not have sunk before 1857.

The ocean is not kind to shipwrecks and the **artifacts** inside them. Waves, bacteria, sea animals, and ocean salts can damage wrecks. In some cases, however, cold temperatures and silt can protect items

Divers sometimes find artifacts within ancient shipwrecks.

from decay. Fragile items such as postcards were found intact at the *Titanic* wreck site.

The study of human activity related to the sea is known as maritime archaeology. This science has grown in the last 50 years as diving equipment has improved. Now divers can explore much deeper areas and stay underwater far longer than they could in the past.

Early divers used diving bells and clumsy helmets to **salvage** wrecks in shallow water. The first scuba equipment was invented in 1943, giving divers more freedom of movement. Today, they wear high-tech scuba gear and breathe special mixed gases that allow them to dive deeper. In order to explore deeper still, people built undersea vehicles called submarines. Miniature submarines called submersibles take humans far below the surface. They can go much deeper than large submarines. Similar machines without people in them, called remotely operated vehicles (ROVs), are connected

Small AUVs can search through shipwrecks that might be dangerous for people to explore.

MORE THAN ARCHAEOLOGY

Biologists also explore shipwrecks to learn more about deep-sea life. Many new types of sea life have been found this way, including deep-sea fish, bacteria, and worms. Scientists who discovered the *Titanic* learned that previously unknown iron-eating bacteria created rusty growths. These growths looked like icicles, leading scientists to name them *rusticles*.

to ships on the surface by cables. An operator on the ship controls them. ROVs carry cameras and robotic arms. They can explore shipwrecks without putting humans in danger. Autonomous underwater vehicles (AUVs) are robot submarines with no cables. They are programmed to follow a certain path under the water and then return to the ship.

Although some divers grab every artifact in sight, professional archaeologists take a different approach. Before touching a site, they draw detailed maps that include natural features such as cliffs and reefs. They also take photos. The next step is to carefully excavate, or dig out the site. Divers use hammers and picks to remove mud and rock. Then they fan the area to remove any last bits of silt and mud. Each item is carefully mapped, measured, and photographed before it is moved. Its position may give clues about how the ship sank and help identify parts of the ship.

Next, divers place small items in plastic or mesh containers. They use ropes, chains, and pulleys to lift larger items. Air-filled bags may be used to lift very heavy objects. The bags float to the surface and are picked up by crews on boats.

Sometimes archaeologists raise a whole ship in order to study it or put it on display. This can take many years. When the Swedish ship *Vasa* was raised, divers tunneled under the ship and passed cables through the tunnels. The cables were floated to the surface, carrying the ship up with them. The *Mary Rose* was also raised. Its hull was wired to a frame and placed in a cradle. A crane lifted the whole cradle onto a waiting ship.

LOCATING SHIPWRECKS

It can be difficult to figure out exactly where a ship sank, especially if it went down long ago. Scientists searching for wrecks use different methods to find them. They may ask fishers where their nets often get snagged. They search marine archives for records of the ship's last known position. More information may be found in survivors' accounts. Once scientists have a good idea of where to start, they use sonar to survey large areas of the seabed. **Magnetometers** show the location of metal objects, even if they are buried. Debris can be found using cameras like the ones Ballard and Michel used when searching for the *Titanic*.

MAKING SHIPS SAFER

Sailors once relied on lighthouses, charts, and their eyes to avoid dangerous reefs and rocks near shore. Lighthouses were kept burning by a keeper who lived on site. Today, lighthouses still warn sailors, but computers rather than people usually control them. Floating **buoys** with lights or foghorns also warn sailors of dangerous coasts.

Even more important today are tools such as radar, which shows the location of objects even in the dark. Radar equipment works by sending out radio waves and

The US Coast Guard places red and green buoys to help ships navigate.

measuring how long it takes them to bounce back. This
makes it possible to know exactly how far away an object
is. The Global Positioning System (GPS) uses a network
of **satellites** in space to make it possible for sailors to
find their exact location on the globe. It also helps
rescuers find survivors when a ship sinks.

New technology helps builders create safer ships.
Computer programs let them extensively test their
designs to make sure they are safe. New types of steel
and other building materials make ships stronger. Ships
can also be made safer through new laws. Laws passed

How GPS Works

GPS is made up of a group of satellites that orbit Earth. They send signals to handheld GPS receivers on land, in the air, and at sea. The signals tell the receivers the exact location of the satellite that sent them. The GPS receivers collect signals from many different satellites. A computer in the receiver then figures out how far away the receiver is from each satellite, telling the receiver its precise location on the planet.

after the *Titanic* sank required ships to carry enough lifeboats for all their passengers and crew.

Science continues to improve rescue technology, leading to more saved lives. Special safety suits can hold body heat in and keep water out. More *Titanic* passengers might have survived with suits like these. Many lifeboats today have roofs to protect passengers from wind and waves. They are stocked with radios, water purifiers, and other survival equipment.

Devices called emergency position-indicating radio beacons are now required on certain US vessels. These beacons are water activated. If a boat sinks, the beacon

Members of the Coast Guard rescue people on ships of all shapes and sizes.

sends information so the Coast Guard can quickly find the survivors. The Coast Guard sends planes, helicopters, and boats to the rescue. Helicopter-based rescue swimmers can be lowered by cable to the boat or water to save lives.

People make mistakes, so it is impossible to prevent all shipwrecks. However, improvements in ship design, navigational tools, safety laws, and rescue equipment have already saved many lives. As we continue to learn from the past, we can use that knowledge to save many more.

TOP FIVE WORST SHIPWRECKS

1. **Wilhelm Gustloff**
   This German ship holds the record for the deadliest shipwreck of all time. A Soviet submarine sank the ship in 1945 during World War II. More than 9,300 people died.

2. **Goya**
   Another German ship, the *Goya*, was sunk by Soviet forces in 1945 while carrying wounded troops and civilians. More than 6,800 people died.

3. **Lancastria**
   Approximately 5,000 people died when the *Lancastria*, a British liner carrying civilians and troops, was bombed by German warplanes in 1940.

4. **General von Steuben**
   A Soviet submarine sank the *General von Steuben* in 1945. It was carrying injured troops and refugees. As many as 4,500 lives were lost.

5. **Doña Paz**
   The *Doña Paz*, a ferry from the Philippines, collided with a tanker ship in 1987. More than 4,300 people were killed. The ferry had been overcrowded.

LEARN MORE

FURTHER READING

Ganeri, Anita and David West. *The Sinking of the Titanic and Other Shipwrecks*. New York: Rosen, 2012.

Stewart, Melissa. *Titanic*. Washington, DC: National Geographic, 2012.

WEB SITES

History Channel—*Titanic* Interactive
http://www.history.com/interactives/titanic-interactive
This interactive Web site features information about the design of the *Titanic*, a map of its route, and a timeline of the sinking.

Nova—Voyage of Doom
http://www.pbs.org/wgbh/nova/lasalle
This Web site takes an in-depth look at the sinking of the French ship *La Belle* in 1686. It also has information about buoyancy and the laws regarding shipwrecks.

GLOSSARY

artifacts (AR-tuh-fakts) objects made by human beings in another time or era

buoyancy (BOI-uhn-see) the force that causes an object to float in a liquid

buoys (BOO-ees) floats marking dangerous waters

decayed (di-KAYD) rotten or broken down

gunports (GUN-ports) the holes in the side of a ship that cannons fire through

hull (HUHL) the shell or body of a ship

keel (KEEL) the structure on the bottom of a boat that keeps it stable

magnetometers (mag-ni-TOM-uh-tuhrz) instruments for detecting the presence of magnetic fields

radar (RAY-dar) equipment that uses radio waves to locate objects

reefs (REEFS) ridges of rocks, sand, and coral close to the surface of the ocean

salvage (SAL-vij) to retrieve items from a shipwreck

satellites (SAT-uh-lites) objects that move in a curved path around a planet

scuba (SKOO-buh) using an air tank and breathing device to dive for long periods of time

sonar (SOH-nar) a tool for finding underwater objects using sound waves

INDEX

ancient shipwrecks, 7–8
archaeologists, 21, 23, 24
Archimedes, 10, 13
artifacts, 20, 23

buoyancy, 10, 12, 13, 16

collisions, 14–15, 30

design problems, 8, 16

hulls, 4, 5, 7, 11–12, 14–15, 16–17, 18, 19, 24

lifeboats, 5, 6, 28

navigation, 8, 29

overloading, 8, 16–17

ship technology, 8–9, 27

Titanic, 4–7, 9, 10, 14, 19, 21, 23, 25, 28

wars, 8, 16, 30